Anger Management

 caring for yourself and others

Dedication
For Hari and Rosa

Anger
Management

caring for yourself and others

Nikki Dhillon Keane

Published by Redemptorist Publications
Wolf's Lane, Chawton, Hampshire, GU34 3HQ, UK
Tel: +44 (0)1420 88222, Fax: +44 (0)1420 88805
Email: rp@rpbooks.co.uk, www.rpbooks.co.uk

A registered charity limited by guarantee
Registered in England 03261721

Copyright © Redemptorist Publications 2019
First published September 2019

Series Editor: Sr Janet Fearns
Edited by Eldred Willey
Designed by Eliana Thompson

ISBN 978-0-85231-549-1

A CIP catalogue record for this book is available from the British Library.

The publisher gratefully acknowledges permission to use the following copyright material:
Excerpts from the *New Revised Standard Version Bible: Anglicised Edition*, copyright © 1989,
1995, Division of Christian Education of the National Council of the Churches of Christ in the
United States of America. Used by permission. All rights reserved.
Excerpts from *The Jerusalem Bible*, copyright © 1966, Darton, Longman & Todd Ltd. and
Doubleday, a division of Random House, Inc. Reprinted by permission.

Every effort has been made to trace copyright holders and to obtain their permission for the
use of copyright material. The publisher apologises for any errors or omissions and would be
grateful for notification of any corrections that should be incorporated in future reprints or
editions of this book.

Printed by Lithgo Press Ltd.,
Leicester, LE8 6NU

Acknowledgements

I would like to thank my family for all the long-suffering support
they have shown me while I was writing this book, and while I was
developing the courses on which it is based. I would also like to thank
the clients I have worked with and the people who have attended the
anger management courses I have facilitated. They have shared their
own experiences with openness and bravery, and I have learnt so
much from them.

Introduction

Anger is a natural emotion and yet it can be the cause of serious problems. I have worked with people who, through anger, have lost relationships and careers, damaged their health and wellbeing and hurt the people around them. Yet, if we were to imagine a world without anger, it would not be a better place. Anger is not something we should try to get rid of. Instead we should only try to control it, so that it does not control us.

Never expressing anger, holding it all inside, can be as problematic as uncontrolled rage. Sometimes it is the quiet, passive person who needs help dealing with anger just as much as the one who is shouting or being aggressive.

As a counsellor, I have worked with many people who have had difficulties dealing with anger, whether it was their own anger or that of someone close to them. Some people have had extremely good reasons to feel angry, having experienced years of abuse. Yet their anger ended up being a source of even more pain and suffering.

Several years ago, I had the opportunity to create an anger management course and later on to develop it for different groups of people. This book is largely based on the material from those courses. I hope it will either help you directly with your own anger, or help you to offer support to someone else who is struggling with anger. It is difficult to control things we don't fully understand, and this book will help you to develop your understanding of the different kinds of anger, and the techniques which help with each of them.

This book is written from the perspective of directly helping the reader with their own anger, but you can also read it and get ideas if you wish to learn how to help someone else. You will get most out of the book if you think about your own attitudes to anger as you read it. It is written from a Catholic perspective, but I hope that people from other faith backgrounds will find it equally helpful.

Learning how to manage your anger can be challenging. You will find that there are times when the techniques aren't working for you, or you don't feel able to use them. When that happens, don't worry. Like so many other things, this is a process that takes time and practice. It may seem like hard work but the rewards are well worth it. I hope that this book can help you to achieve that sense of peace which comes from having a positive relationship with your anger, and understanding how to manage it well.

Never be in a hurry; do everything quietly and in a calm spirit.

Do not lose your inner peace for anything whatsoever, even if your whole world seems upset.

What is anything in life compared to peace of soul?

St Francis de Sales

1

The positive side of anger

Anger itself is neither good nor bad: it is how we behave when we feel angry that can be either positive or negative. It is easy to think that good people never get angry. In fact, without anger, many of the great social changes in history would not have happened. People such as Rev. Martin Luther King Jr, Archbishop Desmond Tutu or Mahatma Gandhi were very angry about the injustice they saw around them. They were able to channel their anger in a positive way so that it became what we call *helpful anger*.

What is helpful anger?

Helpful anger is when your angry behaviour leads to positive results like bringing about social change, or protecting yourself or others from harm.

Examples of helpful anger might be:

- Standing up for yourself if someone is taking advantage of you

- Protecting yourself from harm or ending an abusive relationship

- Joining Amnesty International to help campaign for global human rights

- Joining your local Justice and Peace group

- Writing to your MP about an injustice

- Working to support and empower marginalised communities

- Protecting people from being treated unfairly

- Peaceful protesting

Without helpful anger it would be difficult or impossible to do good in the world. We would ignore or accept the suffering and injustices we see around us. We would not stand up for those who are marginalised or oppressed.

Later in this book we will look at how we can stand up for ourselves in non-aggressive ways using helpful anger.

Recognising helpful and unhelpful anger

A useful way to tell the difference between helpful and unhelpful anger is by its results. Helpful anger leads to positive results, such as safety or social change whereas unhelpful anger leads to negative results like violence, or sometimes to self-harm.

Below are some of the differences between helpful and unhelpful anger:

Helpful Anger	Unhelpful Anger
I feel in control and calm (or sometimes nervous) but never aggressive	I feel aggressive and out of control
I am able to empathise with other people	I have no empathy
I can think clearly	My judgement is impaired
I can communicate effectively	My communication is aggressive and unclear
I improve the situation around me	I make the situation worse or add new problems
I protect myself and others	I may harm myself or others
Positive things happen	Negative things happen

Helpful anger is a force for good that doesn't need to change. Most of this book, therefore, will focus on unhelpful anger. From this point on, unless stated otherwise, whenever I talk about anger I will mean the unhelpful kind.

How does anger affect people?

There is evidence that people who are often angry can be affected in the following ways:

- **Physical health:** People who are angry often have a higher risk of physical illnesses and conditions like high blood pressure, strokes or heart attacks (British Association for Anger Management).

- **Mental health:** Anger can affect your psychological health, leading to stress, depression, self-harm or even suicidal thoughts (MIND).

- **Relationships:** Anger can affect your relationships. One in five people have ended a relationship or friendship because of how someone behaved when they were angry (Boiling Point 2008 Mental Health Foundation).

- **Work:** Anger can affect your career. People who are angry at work are less likely to be promoted and may even lose their job (British Association for Anger Management).

- You are also more likely to end up getting injured or to injure someone else when you are behaving aggressively.

Anger can damage people's lives in significant ways. However, with the right skills and knowledge, it is possible to learn how to control anger and live a more peaceful, healthier and happier life.

2

Beliefs about anger

When we are talking about belief here, we mean it in the psychological sense of the word rather than your spiritual or religious beliefs. Beliefs about anger concern what is acceptable behaviour when you have angry feelings, or whether it is acceptable to have those feelings at all. When we are children, we learn about the world and develop our beliefs by watching the adults around us. People who grew up in a home where anger was expressed by aggression, shouting, swearing, or throwing things are likely to believe that this is a normal way to express anger.

Alternatively, they might have been so distressed by the aggressive behaviour they witnessed that they never express anger themselves.

Conversely, people who were brought up in a home where the adults all held their anger inside, or were told it was wrong to express anger, will probably have grown up finding it difficult to express anger at all. It is likely that these beliefs will also make it challenging for them to cope with other people expressing anger. Couples who have different beliefs about anger can experience difficulties dealing with each other's anger.

People rarely stop to think about their beliefs about anger. However, if you want to improve the way you deal with anger, it can be very helpful to recognise and challenge your own beliefs about what is normal or acceptable angry behaviour.

To help you think about your beliefs about anger, have a look at the statements below and decide which you think are true or false.

- Helpful anger is the only acceptable kind of anger
  true   false

- Good, holy people never feel angry
  true   false

- It is never acceptable to let another person see my anger
  true   false

- Expressing anger shows I really care
  true   false

- It is acceptable to throw or break things as long as no one is hurt
  true   false

- It is acceptable to hit the wall or table in anger
  true   false

- It is acceptable to hit someone if they asked for it
  true   false

- It is acceptable to smack a naughty child in anger
  true   false

- In my own home, I can behave how I want when I am angry
  true   false

Think about your own beliefs about angry behaviour, and try writing them down. As you read through the rest of this book, you may find it helpful to come back to your list and see if your answers change or remain the same.

Our beliefs can affect anger in another way. People with very rigid, inflexible beliefs about the way something should happen can easily become angered when things don't go to plan, or when other people have a different view.

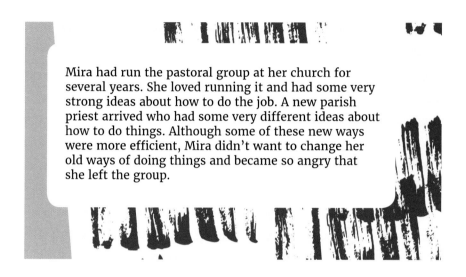

Mira had run the pastoral group at her church for several years. She loved running it and had some very strong ideas about how to do the job. A new parish priest arrived who had some very different ideas about how to do things. Although some of these new ways were more efficient, Mira didn't want to change her old ways of doing things and became so angry that she left the group.

If Mira had been more flexible about how things were done, she would have experienced less anger and would probably have been able to carry on running the group she loved. She may have been able to discuss and compromise on some of the new ideas, some of which might have been very helpful. Developing a more flexible attitude can help to lessen the chances of becoming angry.

Thinking about your own beliefs about what angry behaviour is normal or acceptable, and about how flexible you are able to be, is a first step towards understanding your own relationship with anger.

3

Recognising your anger

Anger can take over your mood with alarming speed. The ability to act as soon as possible is an important part of anger management: the sooner you take action, the easier it is to take control of angry reactions.

Knowing what environmental factors will make it more likely for you to lose your temper can help you to take action in advance of becoming angry.

Factors that make anger more likely

The following are some examples of factors which can make angry reactions more likely.

- Lack of sleep
- Hunger or low blood sugar
- Chronic pain or illness
- Withdrawal from alcohol, nicotine, caffeine or other drugs
- Hormonal changes, caused by puberty, menopause, pregnancy or premenstrual syndrome
- Being under a lot of stress
- Dealing with grief and loss
- Feeling nervous about something

These factors are not excuses for anger; they just make it harder to manage anger.

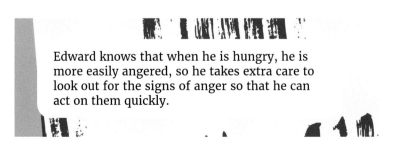

Edward knows that when he is hungry, he is more easily angered, so he takes extra care to look out for the signs of anger so that he can act on them quickly.

You may be familiar with the recommendation to "never go to bed on an argument." While this is often good advice, there are also times when tiredness leads to increased anger and a good night's sleep can make things much easier to deal with in the light of day and after giving yourself time to "cool down".

Awareness of the factors that make anger more likely make it easier to predict those times when you are more likely to lose your temper. It is then possible to prepare yourself by making extra efforts with the techniques that we will be discussing a little later on.

The signs of anger

Anger sends us into fight or flight mode, in the same way that might happen if we were in a dangerous situation. This is a useful response when faced with physical danger, but is less so in most situations of anger. The fight or flight hormones increase oxygen (as your breathing gets quicker) and increase the flow of blood to your organs. The parts of your brain dealing with complex thought and empathy (which you don't need to run away or fight) actually shut down. The small part of your brain that deals with the fight or flight response (the amygdala) takes charge (Griffin and Tyrell, 2008). When that happens, your thoughts become very black and white: "I am one hundred per cent right and you are one hundred per cent wrong."

This can feel as though you have achieved great clarity of thought, because you are so sure that you are right. In fact, it just means that only a tiny part of your brain is working.

All this happens incredibly fast, and once parts of your brain shut down it is very difficult to manage your anger. So the quicker we take action to control our reactions, the better. The most effective way we can do that is to get to know the signs that we are becoming angry. There are signs

- in our thoughts
- in our bodies
- in our behaviours

These differ from person to person, but they often include some of the following:

Signs of anger in our thoughts:

- I am right and you are wrong
- I have to make you see that I am right
- You always/never do this
- This always happens to me
- Why me?
- This is so unfair

Signs of anger in our bodies:

- Breathing and heart rate get quicker
- Tightness in the chest
- Feeling very hot or cold
- Tight muscles
- Feeling dizzy
- Sweating

Signs of anger in our behaviour:

- Clenched fists
- Clenched jaws
- Shouting/raising your voice
- Hitting the wall/banging the table
- Slamming doors
- Throwing things
- Violence
- Silence/sulking
- Storming off

Each person has slightly different signs of anger, so it is worth thinking about what yours are. Getting to know your own signs will help you to recognise your anger so that you can act quickly to manage it. The anger starts in your thoughts, but the signs in your body are likely to be the first that you will notice. By the time the signs of anger in your behaviour appear, it is harder (but not impossible) to take back control.

An angry person might feel as though they are taking control of the situation, but in fact the reverse is true; it is actually their anger that is in control.

4

Three steps to control simple anger

Many people go through life believing that losing your temper is something that is beyond our control. The way we tend to talk about anger only reinforces the idea that something or someone else is responsible for our angry feelings:

"You made me angry."

"That makes me so mad."

In this chapter, we will see that each of us is able to choose whether, and how, we get angry.

Simple anger is the straightforward anger that is a reaction to something that has just happened or that is happening right now. A trigger is something which sparks an angry reaction, for example, a person being rude or treating you badly. Another person's anger can also be a trigger for you.

In order to manage your anger, you need to take control of the anger in your thoughts, body and behaviour. However, we need to work on these in the opposite order to that in which they first appear. You start with taking control of the anger in your behaviour, then the anger in your body and lastly, you are ready to tackle the anger in your thoughts.

Step 1: Controlling the anger in your behaviour: time out

The first thing you need to do is to move away from the trigger so that it doesn't keep triggering your anger. In other words, give yourself some time out.

If you are in a situation with another person who is also angry, they could misinterpret walking away as storming off, so it is important to let the person know what you are doing. When you do this it is helpful to:

- tell the person that you are feeling angry and you are going away to calm down;

- say that you can discuss the issue later when you are calm;

- keep the focus on your own anger, even if the other person is also angry;

- not wait for the other person to give you permission to go: they might want you to stay and argue.

Calming down can take time: the process can last anywhere from five minutes to twenty-four hours or even longer (Greenburger and Padesky, 2016). It is important to use the time effectively to really calm down using the following steps.

Step 2: Controlling the anger in your body: slowing down your breathing

It is not possible to control the anger in your thoughts while the flight or fight hormones are affecting your brain function.

For your brain to become fully functional again, you need to control the effects of the flight or fight hormones in your body. These hormones speed up your breathing and heart rate, so the best way to counteract this is to slow your body down. The most effective way of doing this is to slow down your breathing. Counting as you breathe is a good way to achieve this. Concentrating on counting also helps to distract you from your angry thoughts as you slow down your breathing. It is most helpful to breathe out for longer than you breathe in.

(https://www.nhs.uk/conditions/stress-anxiety-depression/controlling-anger/)

Try counting five as you breathe in and nine as you breathe out, or seven as you breathe in and eleven as you breathe out.

During this step you can also use visualisations to help you calm down: imagine yourself breathing out all of your anger until it disappears, or imagine yourself in a beautiful calm place like a beach, a forest or a garden.

Step 3: Controlling the anger in your thoughts: cool thinking

Once you have controlled the anger in your body, you can start working on your thoughts; but first it is necessary to understand the relationship between thoughts and anger. Most people assume that a trigger leads to an angry reaction:

Trigger → Angry reaction

In fact, it is a little more complicated. It all happens so quickly that it seems as though the reaction is immediate, but it is actually your *thoughts* about the trigger that will lead to an angry reaction or a calm reaction. Hot thoughts lead to angry reactions and cool thoughts lead to calm reactions.

Trigger → Hot thoughts → Angry reaction

Trigger → Cool thoughts → Calm reaction

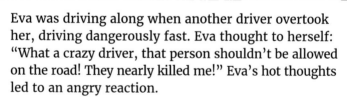

Eva was driving along when another driver overtook her, driving dangerously fast. Eva thought to herself: "What a crazy driver, that person shouldn't be allowed on the road! They nearly killed me!" Eva's hot thoughts led to an angry reaction.

On another occasion, Eva was driving along when the same thing happened, but she had very different thoughts: "Thank goodness I was able to brake quickly enough, so that no one was hurt. Maybe that person is in a hurry for a good reason, like rushing to the hospital." Because Eva had cool thoughts, she reacted to the situation in a calm way, without getting angry.

Another way to think of it, is that hot thoughts will lead you to understand an event in a way that makes you angry, while cool thoughts lead you to understand the situation in a way that leaves you calm.

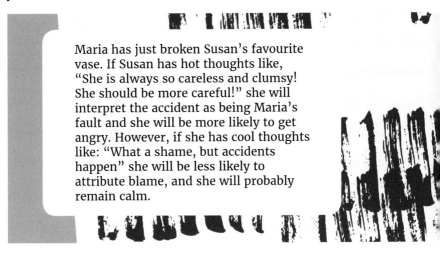

Maria has just broken Susan's favourite vase. If Susan has hot thoughts like, "She is always so careless and clumsy! She should be more careful!" she will interpret the accident as being Maria's fault and she will be more likely to get angry. However, if she has cool thoughts like: "What a shame, but accidents happen" she will be less likely to attribute blame, and she will probably remain calm.

When you understand that it is your thoughts, rather than the trigger, that spark an angry reaction, you can decide to change your thoughts so that you stay calm.

Becoming a cool thinker

It's not always easy to think cool, because the hot thoughts and angry reactions happen so quickly. It can help to prepare some cool thoughts in advance so that they are ready for when you need them. If you have a regular trigger (something which happens often and you tend to get angry every time) then it is extremely helpful to have some cool thoughts at the ready so that you have prepared in advance. The more practice you have of cool thoughts, the easier you will find it to think of new ones.

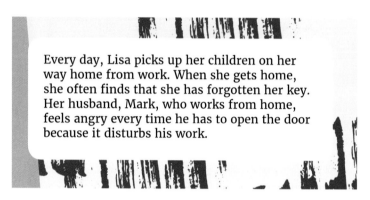

Every day, Lisa picks up her children on her way home from work. When she gets home, she often finds that she has forgotten her key. Her husband, Mark, who works from home, feels angry every time he has to open the door because it disturbs his work.

Because Mark knows that Lisa is likely to forget her keys again, he can recognise his hot thoughts and think of some cool thoughts in advance which will help him to react to the situation in a cool way.

If you think about your regular triggers (things which often happen and make you feel angry) you can recognise your hot thoughts and prepare some cool thoughts ready for the next time it happens.

It can help you to make a chart like the one below.

Trigger	Hot thought	Cool thought

How do I think cool?

Cool thinking can be challenging, but below is a list of things that can help.

1. Empathy

This is the number one route to cool thinking. It is impossible to have hot thoughts if you have empathy with the other person. As soon as you put yourself in the other person's shoes and look at the situation from their perspective, you will find yourself having cool thoughts. I might feel angry about the slow service in a restaurant until I think about how tired the waitresses and waiters must be, the late hours they have to work and the rude customers with whom they have to deal.

If we look back at our previous example of Mark and Lisa, Mark will feel less angry with Lisa if he thinks about all the things she has to remember and all the stress she is under.

> Try asking:
> "What is it like for the other person?"

2. Take responsibility

This doesn't mean taking the blame for everything. It means thinking about what you can do to improve the situation. You might not be able to make things right, but perhaps you can learn from the experience and make sure it never happens again.

Mark might wish that Lisa would be better at remembering her key, but he cannot change her. Focusing on what *she* should change is likely to make him more angry. If he thinks about what *he* can do to improve the situation he is more likely to feel calm. He could remind her to take her key in the morning, or help out in the evening so she has time to pack her bag the night before.

> Try asking yourself:
> "What can I do to improve the situation?"

3. Don't take it personally

When something goes wrong, it is easy to think it is all about you. Taking things personally is a sure path towards hot, angry thinking.

Mark might think that Lisa doesn't bother to remember her key because she doesn't care about him or his work. This is a hot thought. Instead he could think that she doesn't remember her key because she has so many other things to think about and remember, which will help him to keep cool.

> Try asking yourself:
> "Is this really about me?"

4. Think positively

When things go wrong, it can be tempting to exaggerate how bad they are. These negative thoughts will also encourage hot thinking and angry reactions.

For example: "It's not fair!" "This is a disaster!" "Everything is ruined!"

When the doorbell goes, Mark might think: "I've lost my train of thought now because I have been disturbed. Now everything is ruined!" Instead he could think about what is positive about the situation: he has a beautiful family. He can also make sure he keeps a sense of perspective about how much damage it really causes him to get up and open the door.

> Try asking:
> "Is it really that bad?" Or:
> "What is positive about this situation?"

5. Keep to the present

"Always" and "never" are hot words. They instantly turn a thought into a hot thought.

For example, Mark could say: "She never remembers her key!" But that isn't really true, (in fact, she has remembered her key more often than she has forgotten it) and it is a hot thought that will make him angry.

> Try thinking about what is happening right now.

6. Beware of "*should and shouldn't*"

Any words like "must", "should" or "have to", as well as their opposites are also hot words. If you find yourself talking or thinking with these words, you are likely to be having hot thoughts which will lead to anger.

Mark could think: "She should remember her key!" This would be a hot thought. A cooler thought could be: "What would help her to remember her key?"

> Instead of thinking:
> "This shouldn't happen"
>
> try thinking:
> "What could happen instead?"

Hot and cool communication

In the same way that certain words or phrases can create hot and cool thoughts, they can also affect the way we communicate with each other. When we talk to another person using hot words and phrases, it is much more likely to lead to a heated argument.

If we continue the same example on the previous page, Mark has a choice as to how he communicates to Lisa.

Hot Communication	Cool Communication
"You never remember your key! You have ruined my concentration and now I'll never get this work finished."	"I understand how many things you need to remember but I find it a problem when I have to stop working to let you in. What can I do to help you remember your key more often?"

Non-verbal communication is an important part of cool communication. The way we interact with each other relies heavily on body language and tone of voice.

Cool non-verbal communication includes:

- Open, relaxed body language
- Warm, facial expression
- Calm tone of voice

If you are someone who naturally appears aggressive or stressed you may need to work on your non-verbal communication skills. (You can get more information at the centre for nonviolent communication www.cnvc.org)

If the person you are talking to uses hot communication, use the three steps to avoid them becoming a trigger for you.

Step one: Controlling the anger in your behaviour (time out)

Step two: Controlling the anger in your body (slow breathing)

Step three: Controlling the anger in your thoughts (cool thinking)

Cool communication means standing up for yourself in a controlled and respectful way. It does not mean swallowing your anger or being a pushover.

The following are some tips for cool communication:

- Try to keep thinking cool. If you feel yourself becoming angry, use the three steps to help you calm down.

- Keep to saying "I" and talking about how you feel, for example, "I feel upset when that happens" rather than, "You upset me."

- Try to avoid criticising or insulting the other person, for example, "I feel taken for granted when you don't help" rather than, "You are so lazy. You never help!"

- Try to avoid discussing disagreements when you are tired, hungry, or there are other factors present which might make it easier for you to lose your temper.

- Try to give the other person the benefit of the doubt. For example, you can say something like, "I'm sure you never meant to hurt my feelings, but that is what happened."

- Don't feel you have to win.

- Be ready to agree to disagree. There may be some things about which you will always hold different views.

Using the three steps, cool thoughts and cool communication will usually help when you want to manage your anger. However, in the following chapters we will look at some of the ways in which anger can be a little more complicated.

5

Old anger

Sometimes, an angry reaction can take you by surprise because it seems out of proportion for a relatively minor trigger. When this happens, it can be because not all of your anger is about the trigger; some of that anger is "old anger" which you may have been carrying around with you for days, weeks or years.

What is "old anger"?

It can, at times, seem preferable to push anger down inside rather than losing your temper. This can give the impression that you are managing your anger, but in fact you are just holding on to it. It doesn't go anywhere: it just stays inside you where it can do a lot of harm. In chapter 10 we will look at what held-in anger can do to you, but for now we will look at what happens when it comes out in uncontrolled ways as old anger.

Imagine a cupboard that you are filling up with different things. Each time you have something new to add, you open the door and place the item in the cupboard. Because you never take anything out, the cupboard will start to get full. Eventually, there will come a time when you open the door to add something new, and everything will tumble out on top of you.

Old anger is just like that. As you react to the trigger, all the old anger will come out at the same time, giving the impression that all the anger is about that one, small trigger. The three steps to manage simple anger may not work, because we need to manage old anger in a different way.

How to manage old anger

Step 1: Recognition

The first step is to recognise your old anger by including these questions with your cool thoughts:

- Was this reaction really in proportion to the trigger?
- What do I really feel about this trigger?
- What is the rest of my anger about?

Step 2: Release

You can then deal with your old anger by letting it out in a controlled way, which means waiting until you are feeling calm and safe. The middle of an argument, or when you have just been triggered by something new, are not the moments for you to start trying to deal with your old anger.

In some cases you can let out your old anger to the person who made you angry. It can be very healing if you can have a meaningful and helpful conversation with the person who triggered your old anger. However, this is not always possible, because the person:

- would not listen and understand;
- is no longer in your life, or has died;
- would hurt you again if you approached them.

If you are thinking about dealing with your old anger directly with the person who triggered it,

- make sure that it is safe to do so;
- use cool communication and skills;
- think about the kind of response you want to get from them If you need them to understand and apologise in order to make you feel better, then you are giving that person considerable control over your wellbeing. They might genuinely not understand what harm they have caused, or they may choose not to apologise.

In many cases, it will be preferable to release your old anger in ways which do not involve the other person directly.

Below are some ways that can help to achieve that. Find a time and place where you are feeling as safe and secure as possible, and when you are not feeling particularly angry. There are several methods you can choose to safely let out your old anger. It might be a good idea to try a few of them and see what works best for you:

- Talk to a trusted friend or counsellor about your anger.
  This can release the pain that you feel because of your anger.
  Try not to use hot thoughts as this can make your anger worse.

- Write a letter to the person, but don't send it. Instead you can tear it up or burn it and imagine your anger burning away.

- Talk to a photograph or an empty chair, imagining you are talking to that person.

- Let out your anger through art, drawing, painting or sculpting.

- Let the anger out through exercise.

- Imagine your anger drifting off like a balloon. (I used to recommend actually writing a message on a balloon and letting it drift off until I learnt that it was very bad for the environment!)

In years gone by, traditional methods of anger management would encourage people to let out old anger physically, by doing something like hitting a cushion. It is now not recommended to do anything like that because, although the physical exertion may help you to feel better, it can actually make you more likely to want to behave violently because you are practising a violent response to your anger (Griffin and Tyrell, 2008).

Talking can be a much more effective way to let out old anger, but a conversation full of hot thoughts is likely to make angry feelings much worse. It is most helpful to focus on

- Cool thoughts

- Cool communication

- Letting go of your anger (there is more information about this in chapter 11)

Relaxation exercises and meditation can be useful when you are releasing old anger. Some people find mindfulness particularly helpful. There is some information about mindfulness at the end of the book and there are plenty of guided meditations to be found on the Internet, including ones focused on releasing anger.

6

Misdirected anger

Misdirected anger is anger which you direct at someone who is not the real trigger. There are several things which can lead to misdirected anger.

Projection

Projection is when we send or "project" our emotions onto someone else. There are two ways we can project anger onto someone who is not the trigger:

- when someone is really angry with themselves, but they don't want to face it, so project their anger onto someone else (type 1);

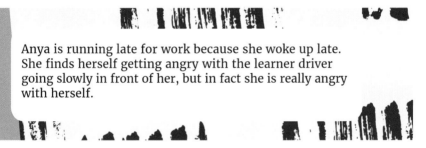

Anya is running late for work because she woke up late. She finds herself getting angry with the learner driver going slowly in front of her, but in fact she is really angry with herself.

- when someone is really angry with another person to whom they can't express anger, so they project the anger onto a third person with whom it feels safer to be angry (type 2).

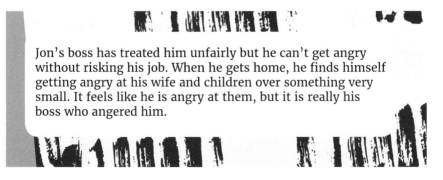

Jon's boss has treated him unfairly but he can't get angry without risking his job. When he gets home, he finds himself getting angry at his wife and children over something very small. It feels like he is angry at them, but it is really his boss who angered him.

Transference

Transference is very similar to the second type of projection, but instead of just projecting a feeling from one person onto another, it involves the whole relationship. With transference, someone redirects all the feelings they have about one person onto a second person. It will usually be because you have a significant or challenging relationship with the original person. If you have feelings of anger about the original relationship, you can transfer this anger onto another person who might look like, or remind you in some way, of the original person.

Alex sometimes talks to Steve in a way that reminds Steve of his father who was a bully. Steve has never been able to talk to his father about how angry he feels about the bullying. Alex is not bullying Steve, but Steve can sometimes suddenly feel really angry with Alex. Steve is not aware that this is happening, and he can't explain why he suddenly gets angry with Alex.

Defensive anger

Defensive anger is a little bit like the first type of projection, except that underneath the anger is a different emotion, usually one which makes you feel vulnerable in some way. In order for you to feel less vulnerable, the real emotion is masked with anger. Examples of some emotions which can be masked by defensive anger are:

- Fear
- Shame
- Guilt
- Nervousness

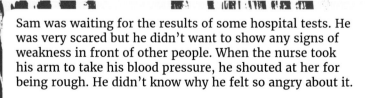

Sam was waiting for the results of some hospital tests. He was very scared but he didn't want to show any signs of weakness in front of other people. When the nurse took his arm to take his blood pressure, he shouted at her for being rough. He didn't know why he felt so angry about it.

How can I stop myself from misdirecting my anger?

These four questions can help you to work out whether you are misdirecting your anger.

To check for projection:
- Is this really my fault?

- Who am I really angry with?

To check for transference:
- Does this person or situation remind me of anyone else?

To check for defensive anger:
- What am I really feeling?

It is helpful to get into the habit of adding these questions to your cool thoughts so that you can regularly check for misdirected anger.

If you recognise defensive anger, the angry feelings will usually fade once you acknowledge the real emotion underneath.

If you recognise that you are really angry with another person, you can deal with that using the three steps for simple anger or your skills for old anger, depending on how recent the trigger was.

If you recognise that you are really angry with yourself, you can do some work on forgiving yourself and making amends. There is information about that in chapter 11.

7

Anger as a symptom of other issues

Anger and stress

When someone finds themselves getting angry more than usual, it could be a sign that they are under stress. With many of us living life at a fast pace, stress is a common problem. Things that can help you deal with stress more effectively include:

- Looking at your work/life balance

- Getting enough sleep

- Regular exercise

- Having a healthy diet, especially avoiding too much caffeine

- Making time for relaxation activities

- Making time for prayer

- Practising Mindfulness

- Talking therapies like counselling or cognitive behavioural therapy (CBT)

There is a link to information about dealing with stress at the end of the book.

Anger and mental health problems

Anger can be a symptom of some mental health problems or personality disorders.

Some mental health problems can include experiences of paranoia which can make people feel very vulnerable. This can lead to angry reactions. Some people can have disturbing, violent thoughts that they can't control, even though they may never act on them.

If you think that you might have a mental health problem, you can talk to your GP. Organisations like MIND can give advice and information to help you or someone else about whom you are concerned. There are contact details at the end of this book.

Anger and grief

People can experience grief as a result of any major loss, like the loss of a job, a relationship, or declining health. Feelings of anger are a natural part of the grief process.

Grief is most often associated with the feelings we have after someone has died. With bereavement, you can experience feelings of anger:

- towards the doctors, nurses and carers;
- towards the illness;
- towards the person who died;
- towards yourself for not having done more;
- towards God for taking that person away or not answering your prayers to let them live.

Some of these feelings of anger can become mixed with feelings of guilt. Sometimes, they can become misdirected towards other people. Talking to a bereavement specialist or a counsellor can help to find ways to work through grief and express anger without hurting others. There is information at the end of the book about where to find support.

You can also use the anger management techniques in this book to help manage any anger that may be causing problems.

If you are supporting someone through bereavement, it is important to allow them space to express all their feelings, including anger, without judgement, and to let them know that all of these feelings are a perfectly normal part of the grief process.

8

Anger and control

In life there are some things we have the power to control or change, and there are others we have no control over. Surprisingly few of us actually take the time to figure out the difference, which leads to wasted time and energy as we work on the things that are out of our control. This will naturally create feelings of frustration and anger. One way to feel less angry is to become more aware and accepting of what you can and cannot control.

Some of the things I can control are:

- My temper

- The things I say

- My actions

- How I choose to spend my spare time

- What I eat and how I look after my body

Some of the things I can't control are:

- Other people's behaviour and life choices

- Other people's emotions and thoughts

- Unexpected life events such as accidents

- Death and illness (particularly illnesses not related to lifestyle)

- Big events such as natural disasters or acts of terrorism

Circles of control

A useful tool that can help build awareness of what you can and cannot change, is called "circles of control." Think of three concentric circles.

In the centre is the circle where you write down all the things you can directly control.

The next circle is where you write down all the things you can influence but not control. "Influence" might mean campaigning for change or justice, or giving someone advice. If you believe in the power of prayer, it could be praying about something.

The largest circle contains things over which you have no control. This can be the most challenging to fill in, because a number of these things might be ones we would like to have some control over. For example, it would be nice to think that we could keep ourselves and our loved ones safe from harm. But the fact is that over many of these things we have absolutely no control at all. We may choose to influence some good causes by donating or campaigning, but it is impossible to do that for every good cause, so there will be some things we choose to leave in our largest circle, trusting that other people are influencing those particular issues.

"People who focus on the things they can control or influence are not only calmer, they have been found to be more successful."

(The *Seven Habits of Highly Effective People,*
Stephen R. Covey)

Circles of control

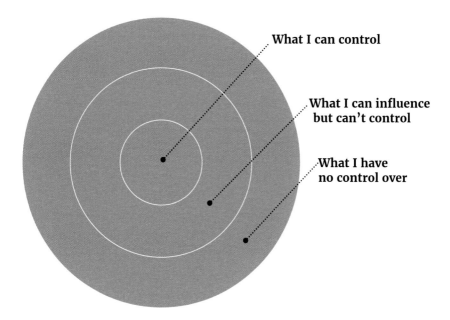

What I can control

What I can influence
but can't control

What I have
no control over

When you recognise what belongs in each circle, the important next step is to let go of all the things you can't control. This can be challenging. Some people find the following strategies helpful:

- Focusing on the things in their central circle which they can control.

- Thinking about what influence they may or may not have, and where that influence ends. For example, you can give someone advice, but once that has been done you will need to let go of your desire to control the outcome.

- Using meditation and breathing exercises. Relaxation exercises and mindfulness are helpful tools.

- Praying about the things they cannot control and leaving them in the hands of God.

Dealing with controlling people

Controllers, or people who wish to control others, focus on the things in their outer circle, to the detriment of concentrating on things like self-control, in their inner circle. This means that people who try to control those around them are likely to get frustrated and angry often and, if they are ignoring their inner circle, won't have a sense of self-control, or know how to control their temper.

You can recognise a controller because they usually:

- are very inflexible – find it difficult to change their plans;

- tend to get angry when they don't get their own way;

- have very little empathy;

- will not admit that they are wrong.

If you think that you might be a controller, talking therapies can help you to let go of the urge to control others and focus on self-control.

Living with a controller can be extremely difficult, not least because they often don't recognise that they are causing the problem. If you are struggling to deal with a controller in your life, you might need support like counselling.

Dealing with aggressive people

Dealing with aggressive people can be dangerous. Your personal safety should always be the first concern.

There are several, very different reasons why someone might behave aggressively. They may have a problem managing their anger; they may have a mental health problem, or personality disorder, or they may be abusive. Aggression can be verbal or physical, but both can be very frightening.

Below are some ideas of how to deal with people who are aggressive.

Keep yourself calm

This is the most important thing you can do when someone else is being aggressive. Aggressive people can sometimes try to trigger your anger deliberately in order to get a response from you. The three steps to help you control simple anger (see chapter 4) and cool thoughts (see chapter 5) can help you remain calm.

It is never helpful to argue with an angry person. Because they are in a state of "fight or flight" they will not be able to see an alternative point of view; instead they are likely to become more aggressive.

Use cool communication

Avoid using hot words and phrases, and be aware of your body language, facial expression and tone of voice (see chapter 5).

Get away from the situation if you can

Try to make sure that you have a clear exit; stay closer to the door than the other person. If you can get away safely it is best to do so, but be careful that the other person doesn't follow you. If possible, keep your phone with you at all times so that you can call for help if necessary.

Keep your distance

It can be dangerous to approach an aggressive person. It is safest to make sure that you stay more than arm's length away in case the other person lashes out. Look around you for anything that could be used as a weapon. Be particularly careful if you are in a place like a kitchen which is full of potentially dangerous objects.

Trust your instincts

If you feel that you are in an unsafe situation, don't stay to try to sort things out. Get away as soon and as safely as you can.

Remember that you have the right to be safe and to be spoken to respectfully

You have the right to remove yourself from any situation that makes you feel threatened or unsafe, even if that means ending a relationship. If you are in a close relationship with a partner, spouse or family member and you often feel threatened or controlled, you may be in an abusive relationship. If that is the case, the information below could be very important for you.

Remember that you are never responsible for another person's aggressive behaviour

We are all responsible for our own behaviour. Someone might say to you, "You made me angry" but, as we have seen, it is the way someone thinks about a situation that can lead to an angry or calm response.

Anger and domestic abuse

Perpetrators of domestic abuse often give the impression that they have an anger management problem but, in spite of appearances, this is often not the case. Many authorities suggest that they are usually much more in control than they seem to be.

Victims and survivors of domestic abuse have described their attackers looking wild and out of control, but at the same time having enough self-control to make sure they only hit their victim in places which will be hidden from view.

If someone has an anger problem, they are likely to lose control of their tempers with their friends, at work, and in all their relationships. In contrast, those who perpetrate domestic abuse are often charming with other people: their aggressive behaviour is directed solely at their victim(s). Rather than a loss of control, aggression can be a tool with which perpetrators control their victims.

For this reason, experts in the field of domestic abuse do not advise anger management as an appropriate kind of support for perpetrators of domestic abuse. Instead, they recommend specialist perpetrator programmes. There is information about how to find them at the end of this book.

This doesn't mean, however, that there is no place for anger management training in the context of domestic abuse. Victims and survivors often have huge amounts of anger about their mistreatment and sometimes go for years without any safe way of expressing it. Expressing anger in front of their perpetrator can be extremely dangerous, yet holding it inside can lead to serious problems. Learning anger management skills can help victims deal with their anger in ways that help to keep them safe. It can also help survivors to move forwards and let go of their anger. There is information in chapter 11 about letting go of anger.

Domestic abuse is not just about physical violence: abuse can be psychological, emotional, sexual, economic or spiritual. It is about one person having control over another. It is extremely serious and can be fatal. If you think you or someone you know might be experiencing domestic abuse you can contact organisations for information and support. There is information at the end of this book.

There is more information about how to recognise domestic abuse, and how to offer safe and appropriate support to victims and survivors in *Domestic abuse in Church communities: a safe pastoral response* which is available in this Pastoral Outreach Series.

9

Helpful anger – standing up for what is right without losing your temper

Most people have a very good reason for becoming angry: there has been some kind of injustice. When this happens, it can be difficult to stand up for what is right. It may seem as though the only options are to:

- passively accept the injustice and keep the anger held inside;

- let anger out in inappropriately aggressive and uncontrolled ways.

Both of these are examples of unhelpful anger. The most successful way to stand up for justice, as we saw in chapter 1, is with helpful anger. In this chapter we will look at some ways in which we can use helpful anger through:

- Non-aggressive assertiveness

- Creating strong boundaries

Non-aggressive assertiveness skills

Many people find assertiveness very challenging. Some people try to avoid confrontation of any kind, particularly if they have been brought up to be passive.

Many of us have been taught to "turn the other cheek", in other words, not to retaliate when attacked or insulted. This could give the impression that we should simply accept injustice – which is far from being either correct or appropriate when a situation is so serious that action is necessary and possibly lifesaving.

If you are in a situation which is unjust, but you can't stand up for yourself effectively, you may find that:

- you hold in your anger until it all bursts out one day at a small trigger (old anger);

- you project your anger onto someone else with whom it is easier to express anger (misdirected anger);

- you hold your anger inside where it can be damaging (we will have a look at held-in anger in chapter 10).

Some people may become aggressive when standing up for themselves. Often, they will not recognise that this is a problem, but their behaviour will be difficult for the people around them.

Aggression is rarely the most successful way to assert yourself. Non-aggressive assertiveness is usually a much more effective way of standing up for what is right.

The following are examples of non-aggressive assertiveness skills:

- Cool thinking and cool communication skills

- Respect and empathy: for example, "I can see that you are all very busy but could I talk to a member of staff please?"

- Respectful but firm ways to say "no." It can help to prepare some in advance, for example:
  - Now is not a good time for me
  - I'm not able to do that
  - I can't accept this

- The "broken record" technique, where you just calmly and politely repeat what you want to say until someone takes notice, for example: "This item is damaged; I would like a refund, please."

A word of caution: assertiveness and abuse

Assertiveness is a positive thing, but if you are living with abuse and it feels unsafe to assert yourself, trust your instincts. There is information in chapter 8 about anger and domestic abuse.

Boundaries

One of the most important things you can do to protect yourself from people taking advantage is to have strong boundaries.

We all live with rules:

- the law – telling us what we are and are not allowed to do;
- social norms – telling us how to live peacefully with each other;
- religious faith – offering guidance on how to live well.

Boundaries are like the personal rules we create which help us to live safely. People who don't have strong boundaries can find that other people take advantage of them often. This can lead to frequent feelings of anger, whether or not it is expressed outwardly.

We all have basic rights – including you. For example:

You have the right to be treated fairly

You have the right to be safe

You have the right to get what you pay for

You have the right to say "no" to something you don't want to do

You have the right to be treated with respect

You have the right to be listened to

You have the right to choose your own faith or beliefs

Some of your rights are protected by law (for example, your right not to be attacked) while others (such as your right to be listened to) are not. These rights show us where to set boundaries.

Each person will have their own unique set of boundaries. One person might have strong views about something which doesn't bother another person, and find something completely fine which the other person finds unacceptable.

Your boundaries are also your personal limitations. We would all like to feel as though we had limitless resources, practical, psychological and spiritual, with which we could offer unending help and support to anyone. The fact is that we all have to live within our human limitations, and there are times when we have to draw the line.

For example, we may wish to be of help to homeless people. We might donate to organisations which support homeless people. We might buy a copy of *The Big Issue*, or buy a cup of tea and a sandwich for someone sleeping on the street. We might sit and talk with them. But most of us would stop short of inviting someone to come and live in our house.

Knowing what your boundaries are makes it very much easier to keep them strong. It is difficult when someone puts you on the spot by asking for something and you are not sure whether you think it is fair or acceptable. If you want to be able to stand up for yourself or stand up for justice, it is helpful to work out as many of your personal rules as possible in advance.

Have a look at these. Which, if any, feel like reasonable requests and which feel like someone is trying to take advantage of you?

How do you feel about a friend asking you to:

- lend them £50?

- lend them £50 when they didn't pay you back last time?

- stay at your house for an indefinite period of time?

- help them to cover up a crime?

- help them to do something you believe is immoral?

If you find some things unacceptable, how would you say no? If the idea of saying no feels difficult or stressful, it is a sign that you need stronger boundaries. You can use non-aggressive assertiveness skills (for example your ways to say "no" effectively) to help make your boundaries stronger.

If you strengthen your boundaries, you may find that:

- other people treat you with more respect;

- you are more focused on your internal circle of control;

- you become angry less frequently;

- you don't need to hold anger inside because you are dealing directly with situations that could become triggers.

10

What happens if you don't deal with anger?

We have already seen that unhelpful anger can harm health, relationships and careers when it comes out in aggressive or violent ways. Anger that is not properly dealt with can also manifest itself in other ways.

Passive aggression

If someone doesn't want to admit that they are really angry, they might express their anger as passive aggression. A passive aggressive person might be absolutely convinced that they feel fine, but their anger is coming out in underhand ways. A lot of this will happen subconsciously, so that the person doesn't realise what is going on.

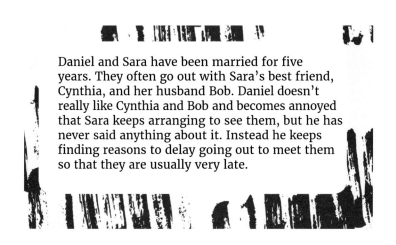

Daniel and Sara have been married for five years. They often go out with Sara's best friend, Cynthia, and her husband Bob. Daniel doesn't really like Cynthia and Bob and becomes annoyed that Sara keeps arranging to see them, but he has never said anything about it. Instead he keeps finding reasons to delay going out to meet them so that they are usually very late.

Passive aggression can be a problem because it leads you to avoid any opportunity to face the issue that has triggered anger and to deal with it head-on. It can also create difficulties when someone feels the aggression behind an action or words but the first person denies there is any anger there.

If you think you might be passive aggressive sometimes, it can help to think about expressing "helpful anger", using non-aggressive assertiveness and boundaries, which can help you deal with triggers in a more direct and helpful way.

If you have held in anger for a long time, look at the ways to release old anger (see chapter 5). Support like counselling can help you to get in touch with your feelings. Living with someone who is passive aggressive can be difficult, and counselling can also support you if your spouse or partner is unwilling or unable to seek help to change.

Chronic Anger

When someone has chronic anger, they are always just a step away from losing their temper, often in a way that is out of proportion to the trigger. They have some level of anger all the time. Chronic anger can cause serious problems for your physical and emotional health as well as for the people around you.

Some people have chronic anger because they have been exposed to so many triggers that they are permanently on the alert, continually looking for triggers. When someone has a history of being criticised or treated unfairly, they are more likely to interpret something as critical or unfair, even if it is not meant that way. Something quite innocent may remind them of things that made them angry in the past – which turns that thing into another trigger.

People with chronic anger usually have large amounts of old anger, but because they are so easily triggered, it can be difficult to release the old anger without triggering an angry reaction.

If you have chronic anger, it can help to talk to a professional such as a counsellor, cognitive behavioural therapy (CBT) practitioner, or anger management specialist. Living with someone who has chronic anger can be very difficult. If the person you live with has chronic anger but won't get help, it can be beneficial for you to talk to a counsellor yourself, to help find ways to deal with the stress of living with someone who has so much anger.

It is easy to mistake a perpetrator of domestic abuse for someone with chronic anger. This can lead to someone being sent for anger management treatment when what they actually need is a programme for perpetrators.

- Most perpetrators focus their aggression towards their victim(s), and are charming with other people. Someone with chronic anger usually gets angry with everyone. However, anyone attacking or behaving abusively with their spouse or partner is perpetrating domestic abuse, whether or not they are also aggressive with other people.

- A perpetrator of abuse uses aggressive behaviour as a tool to control their victim(s). Someone with chronic anger does not use anger to control other people.

- Abuse does not come from feelings, like anger. It comes from attitudes and values. (Lundy Bancroft, *Why Does He Do That?: inside the minds of angry and controlling men*, 2002.) A perpetrator of abuse has a belief that they are superior to their victim and that they are entitled to treat them abusively.

- Someone who is using aggression abusively should get help from specialist perpetrator programmes, not from anger management programmes.

- Some people feel angry all the time because they are living with abuse. If you think that is why you feel angry, you should get specialist help as soon as possible.

Anyone who suspects that they might be being abused, even if the abuse is not physical, should get help straight away, whether or not the perpetrator is willing to get help.

There is more information about anger and domestic abuse in chapter 8 and information about getting help at the end of this book.

Internalised anger

You may know people who never appear to be angry. There could be many reasons for this, including the following:

- They are very good at cool thinking so that very little bothers them.

- Their anger is usually the helpful kind which doesn't look like the kind of anger we recognise.

- They are very good at managing their anger and dealing with it swiftly.

- Their anger has been internalised.

Internalised anger is a common problem for people who:

- have been brought up with the belief that it is always wrong to feel or express anger;

- cannot express their anger safely, for example, if they are living with someone who is abusive.

Internalised anger is held inside until it starts to affect the angry person. It can lead to feelings of depression and low confidence. It can also lead to self-destructive behaviours, self-harm or even suicidal thoughts and feelings. If it is left to build up for a long time it can be extremely serious and even dangerous.

Internalised anger can be hard to recognise because the person doesn't appear to be angry. Often a person with internalised anger will look (and feel) more depressed than angry. It is often when they seek help for their low mood that it becomes apparent that they are actually holding onto considerable anger.

If you, or someone you know, has internalised anger, it is extremely important to find ways to express it safely. The skills for dealing with old anger (see chapter 5) can be helpful in letting anger out, but sometimes it is too deeply buried for the angry person to be able to access it alone. Talking therapies like counselling or psychotherapy can help people to deal with their difficult feelings and get in touch with the anger causing them.

Why we hold onto anger

There are several reasons why people hold onto their anger rather than dealing with it:

- **They don't know how to deal with anger safely and effectively**
  As we have seen, there are several techniques which can help people to deal with different kinds of anger in safe and effective ways.

- **They don't feel able to express anger safely**
  If you or someone you know can't express anger because you are living with someone who makes you feel unsafe, it is very important to get help as soon as possible. There is information at the end of this book about where to get help.

- **They imagine that if they let out any anger it will all come flooding out uncontrollably and never stop**
  This is a common fear which stops people from dealing with their anger. It can help to use the skills for getting rid of old anger. Rather than dealing with all the anger at once, you can deal with it in manageable segments. For example, you can write a letter about one specific thing you are angry about, rather than trying to deal with everything at once. Talking therapies or anger management specialists can help.

- **They believe that their anger will keep them safe from people who treat them badly**
  Anger can give you the impression of being strong and powerful because:

  - you are experiencing defensive anger (see chapter 6 on misdirected anger);

  - you are intimidating other people with aggressive behaviour;

  - anger makes you feel like you are standing up for yourself when someone mistreats you.

In fact, constantly expressing anger is more likely to harm you than keep you safe. But it can be tempting to hold onto anger as a way of protecting yourself against mistreatment. If you are being mistreated then stronger boundaries and non-aggressive assertiveness skills will be more helpful than constantly expressing anger.

- **They have become used to their anger**
  When you have been angry for a very long time, the angry feelings, thoughts and behaviours start to feel normal. This can be a problem, not only because you don't notice the signs of anger, but because your body is flooded with the fight or flight hormones associated with anger, which can cause serious problems for your physical and emotional health.

  If you feel angry so often that you are used to your anger, you will probably have large amounts of old anger. You could have chronic anger, so that you feel angry all the time. Talking therapies or an anger management course can help you to recognise and work through your anger.

Desiderata

Go placidly amid the noise and haste, and
remember what peace there may be in silence.

As far as possible, without surrender, be on
good terms with all persons.

Speak your truth quietly and clearly; and listen
to others,

even to the dull and ignorant; they too have
their story...

Therefore be at peace with God, whatever you
conceive him to be.

And whatever your labours and aspirations,
in the noisy confusion of life,

keep peace in your soul. With all its sham,
drudgery and broken dreams,

it is still a beautiful world. Be cheerful.
Strive to be happy.

Max Ehrmann

11

Forgiveness and letting go

We have seen that holding onto anger can be damaging to you and, at times, to the people around you. Forgiveness is a way of letting go of anger and choosing peace. It is putting all the hurt behind you and moving forwards with only positive feelings. Wonderful as that sounds, the idea of forgiving someone can be extremely challenging for some people because:

- **They fear that forgiveness means that what happened was OK**
  Many people hold onto anger because they feel that the person who hurt them does not deserve to be forgiven; or that in some way forgiving them will mean that the hurt was acceptable.

  In fact, forgiving someone certainly doesn't mean that we accept what they have done, and is not something we only do for people who deserve it. The person you forgive does not need to apologise or show repentance for what they have done. They don't even have to know that you forgive them. Forgiveness is something we really do for ourselves so that we can be free of all the pain that comes with holding onto anger.

- **They fear that forgiveness means that the hurt could happen again**
  Forgiveness does not mean that we are laying ourselves open to being hurt over and over again. As we shall see with the different kinds of forgiveness, it is possible to forgive someone at the same time as protecting yourself and making sure that you can't be hurt again.

Different kinds of forgiveness

As Christians, we are taught to forgive our neighbour, no matter what has been done to us, and no matter how many times it is done to us.

> "Then Peter came and said to him, 'Lord, if another member of the church sins against me, how often should I forgive? As many as seven times?' Jesus said to him, 'Not seven times, but, I tell you, seventy-seven times.'"
>
> *Matthew 18:21-22*

As we have seen, the idea of forgiveness can be challenging for several reasons, not least of which could be because letting go of our anger can make us feel vulnerable to being hurt again.

Below are different kinds of forgiveness, which make it possible to let go of anger and at the same time keep ourselves safe. Forgiveness is not always something you can achieve immediately: it is a process that can sometimes take a while. For each kind of forgiveness there is a suggestion of something you can say when you are forgiving the other person. It is possible to say it to the other person directly, but you do not have to. If it is difficult or inappropriate to talk to the person, or if they would not understand, then all you need to do is to say the words to yourself in your head or out loud. The effect can be just as powerful.

Forgive and forget

This is what most people think of when they talk about forgiveness; that you forget the hurt ever happened and carry on with the relationship exactly the same as it was before. You make a decision to trust the person you forgive not to hurt you again.

This kind of forgiveness is appropriate for minor kinds of hurt, or for when the person who hurt you understands what they have done and is really repentant.

Karen said something that really hurt Ali's feelings. Ali spoke to her about it, and when Karen realised how she had hurt Ali, she felt very sorry and promised not to do it again. Ali felt confident to forgive and forget, believing that Karen really was sorry and would not do it again.

What you can say: "You hurt me when you
_____. It made me feel_____.
I forgive you for doing that. To me it is as if it never happened."

Forgive and protect

This is a way to forgive someone you can't really trust not to hurt you again. You can choose to forgive the person but you don't carry on exactly the same as before. You create a new boundary or protection that helps to make sure that you are safe.

Sometimes it takes a while to achieve this kind of forgiveness because you need to work on converting unhelpful anger into the helpful kind and to think about what kind of boundaries will make you feel safe, before you are ready to forgive. It is helpful to see working through your anger as part of the process leading you towards forgiveness.

> Jane and her friend Alison went out for the evening with Alison's new friend Liz. Alison and Jane left the room for a while and when they came back Jane realised that Liz had taken £10 out of her purse. Jane struggled with anger at what Liz had done, but eventually decided to forgive Liz. She felt no more anger or negativity towards Liz. However, the next time they went out, she kept her handbag with her all the time so that Liz was never alone with her bag again.
>
> What you can say: "You hurt me when you_____.
> It made me feel _____. I forgive you,
> I let go of all the anger I felt towards you, but I am making sure that you can never hurt me like that again."

Letting go of the anger and the relationship

This kind of forgiveness is for serious hurt, like abuse, where it is not safe to be in a relationship with that person any longer because they will definitely hurt you again if they have the chance. Sometimes someone may have hurt you so badly that their very presence is a cause of distress and hurt.

In order to forgive people like this, it may be necessary to cut off the whole relationship so that the person is no longer a part of your life before you feel able to let go of your anger. This is a process which can take a long time and sometimes it can help to have someone to talk to like a counsellor or a priest.

Sheena's boyfriend had abused her for three years. She kept ending the relationship but each time he would keep apologising, promising to change and begging for forgiveness. She would return but every time she returned, the abuse would start again. She felt consumed with anger about the abuse, which was causing her great suffering. Eventually she decided the only way forward was to cut him out of her life completely and to let go of the anger.

What you can say: "You hurt me when you_____.
It made me feel_____. I no longer wish to carry all this anger and bitterness. I am handing it back to you, and now both you and the anger are out of my life forever. You are no longer my (partner/friend/brother/sister/parent). I do not wish you harm. I do not wish for revenge. I let go of all of that. I choose peace."

The other person does not have to hear these words; they are just as powerful if you say them to yourself.

You can say these things:

- talking to yourself;

- talking to an empty chair, imagining the person is there;

- talking to a photograph of the person;

- writing it in a letter which you don't send;

- as a prayer.

"Letting go of the anger and the relationship" is an extreme approach, which is necessary if there has been serious abuse, or if the relationship is too dangerous to continue. A less radical option for potentially harmful relationships is "forgive and protect" described above, where the relationship can continue, but with additional boundaries for protection.

All these options for letting go of anger and forgiving the person who hurt you will allow you to live free of anger. This benefits your emotional and physical health. It can leave you feeling at peace with yourself, with God and with the world.

Once you have let go of the anger you had been holding onto, you can live more easily, in a new way, where you choose cool ways of thinking and communicating and have more awareness of how your behaviour affects the people around you.

Forgiving yourself

Sometimes you are the one who is feeling guilty, and who may be at fault. It is necessary to forgive yourself so that you can really feel the forgiveness of another person or the forgiveness of God.

Feelings of guilt that are not dealt with can lead to defensive anger, or to low self-esteem or depression, so it is important to recognise those feelings and forgive yourself. That does not mean ignoring guilt or telling yourself that whatever you have done was fine; as we shall see there is a process here which can take time.

Before looking at the process of self-forgiveness, the very first step is to work out whether there is anything to forgive.

The first question to ask is:

- **"Is this really my fault?"**

If the answer is "no" then you might want to look at why you are feeling guilty. Some people have a tendency to take on too much responsibility for things that are not their fault, while others have a tendency to blame others rather than themselves. Whichever way you are doesn't make you a good or bad person, but it is helpful to recognise these tendencies in ourselves so that we know what to look out for in our own behaviour.

Sometimes people take on inappropriate guilt because the other person is projecting it onto them. Other times, it can just be easier to blame yourself than another person for something.

If it is difficult to work out whether something really is your fault, you can ask yourself:

- **"If another person were in my shoes, would I blame them?"**

If the answer is "no" then it means that your feelings of guilt are inappropriate. Once you have realised that something is not your fault, you can let go of the feelings of guilt; there is nothing to forgive.

However, if you realise that you have done something wrong, you may need to do some work before you feel able to forgive yourself. Ask yourself:

- **"Is there anything I can do to make things right again?"**

If there is anything you can do to put right what you have done wrong, you will probably need to do that before you can move forwards and forgive yourself.

There may be times, however, when what you have done cannot be put right. If that is the case, you will need to ask:

- **"What can I do to make up for it?"**

You may feel that doing something good or helpful will in some way make up for the wrong you have done, so that you can forgive yourself.

You could:

- do something else to help the person who was hurt;

- make a donation to charity;

- do some voluntary work;

- do something to help another person.

Whatever you decide to do will need to be in keeping with the seriousness of what you have done. How far did you go against your own values? How much hurt did you cause another person to feel? These are difficult questions.

For Catholics, the sacrament of reconciliation can help people on their journey towards self-forgiveness as well as offering an opportunity for receiving the forgiveness of God through penance. Whether or not we have access to this sacrament, we can think about things we can do to make up for the thing we did wrong.

Whether you are forgiving yourself or someone who hurt you, forgiveness can be a long process, depending on the nature of the hurt. But whatever it is that you are forgiving, whichever kind of forgiveness is involved, and however long it takes, forgiveness is choosing peace over anger.

12

Living in a new way: choices and consequences

Now that you understand your anger, it is possible for you to make choices that may not have been open to you before you read this book. You will be more aware of how your anger affects not only you, and your physical and emotional health, but also those around you. It is often the people closest to us who are most affected by our anger; the people we love the most who end up getting hurt.

Through understanding anger in a new way, it is possible to choose new ways of thinking and behaving so that you can react in calmer, more controlled ways and let go of the anger that has been weighing you down.

The following sentences can be a helpful way to review your new understanding of your anger and the way you behave around other people.

Before, I reacted angrily to_____

Now, my reaction is _____

Before, when someone hurt me I would_____

Now, when someone hurts me I_____

The way I thought the anger affected the people around me was ___

_____

The way my anger actually affected the people around me was_

_____

The way I want people around me to feel is _____

The way I thought my anger affected me was_____

The way my anger actually affected me was_____

The way I want to feel is_____

Before, my angry hot thoughts were_____

Now, my calm cool thoughts are_____

Before, I thought anger was_____

Now, I know that anger is _____

As you continue your anger management journey, you will need to keep working at the techniques described in the book. There may be times when you slip up, or forget to use them, and feel like you have gone back to square one, but don't give up. Like so many things, anger management takes time and practice. Keep at it and you will get there in the end.

If you wish to continue learning about anger management there are some links on the following pages that you may find helpful. You may also find that talking to a counsellor, CBT practitioner or another kind of therapist who specialises in anger management will help you to continue your journey.

However you choose to continue from here I wish you a life of greater happiness and peace for yourself and for those around you.

Opposite are some prayers which you may find helpful.

A prayer for releasing anger...

Lord, help me to release these feelings of anger. Help me to avoid misdirecting my anger back at myself or out at others who have done no wrong. May it evaporate as I offer my anger up to you.

Help me to make peace with my anger and know that it is a normal emotion that can be used positively to help fuel change.

Help me to change my situation so that, as I am healed, I need not get so angry like this again.

In you I place my love and trust. Amen.

A prayer for forgiveness...

Lord, help me to forgive all those who have hurt me.

May I forget any minor transgressions and move on positively.

May I forgive any hurt or abuse and may you help me to create stronger boundaries to protect myself from any further ill-treatment.

When in danger, help me to escape, forgive and let go of the past from a new place of safety.

Grant me the gift of discernment, so that I may know the difference between situations where I should stay and ones where I should leave.

Guide me to safety, healing and security so that I can begin again and build the self and the life that you want for me. Help me to feel the light of your love and may it guide me each step of my way.

Forgive me for not valuing myself and not realising that I am your child and that you have a wonderful plan for me. Guide me to stay on my path and not allow others to derail me. Help me to see myself through loving eyes as you do.

Help me to see that this forgiveness will set me free from my past and clear the path to my new life!

May your will be done. Amen.

These prayers were written by Michelle Georgia and appear here with her permission.

Resources and further reading

For anger management support and information

NHS Moodzone information on anger: https://www.nhs.uk/conditions/stress-anxiety-depression/controlling-anger/

NHS anger management courses: Contact your GP to find out if one is available in your area

MIND information on anger: https://www.mind.org.uk/information-support/types-of-mental-health-problems/anger/

MIND anger management courses: Contact your local MIND to find out if they run an anger management course https://www.mind.org.uk/information-support/local-minds/

Information on talking therapies and support

NHS information on (CBT Cognitive Behavioural Therapy): https://www.nhs.uk/conditions/cognitive-behavioural-therapy-cbt/

For private CBT: www.babcp.com

NHS information on counselling: https://www.nhs.uk/conditions/counselling/

For private counselling and psychotherapy: www.bacp.co.uk/

NHS information on mindfulness: https://www.nhs.uk/conditions/stress-anxiety-depression/mindfulness/

To find a mindfulness teacher: https://bemindful.co.uk/

There are also many guided meditations to be found online, including ones for releasing anger.

Support for people with anger issues due to bereavement

Cruse bereavement support: https://www.cruse.org.uk/

NHS Moodzone coping with bereavement: https://www.nhs.uk/conditions/stress-anxiety-depression/coping-with-bereavement/

Support and information for people with mental health problems

MIND information about different mental health problems: https://www.mind.org.uk/information-support/types-of-mental-health-problems/mental-health-problems-introduction/

MIND helping someone seek help for a mental health problem: https://www.mind.org.uk/information-support/guides-to-support-and-services/seeking-help-for-a-mental-health-problem/helping-someone-else-seek-help/

NHS information on mental health services: https://www.nhs.uk/using-the-nhs/nhs-services/mental-health-services/

Support for victims and survivors of domestic abuse

The national domestic violence helpline: 0808 2000 247 http://www.nationaldomesticviolencehelpline.org.uk

Women's aid: https://www.womensaid.org.uk/

Refuge: https://www.refuge.org.uk/

Respect (for male victims of domestic violence): http://respect.uk.net/information-support/male-victims-of-domestic-violence/

Information on programmes for people who behave abusively

Respect: http://respect.uk.net